REAL-LIFE
MONSTERS
OF THE DEEP

THE WORLD'S
WEIRDEST
WATER DWELLERS

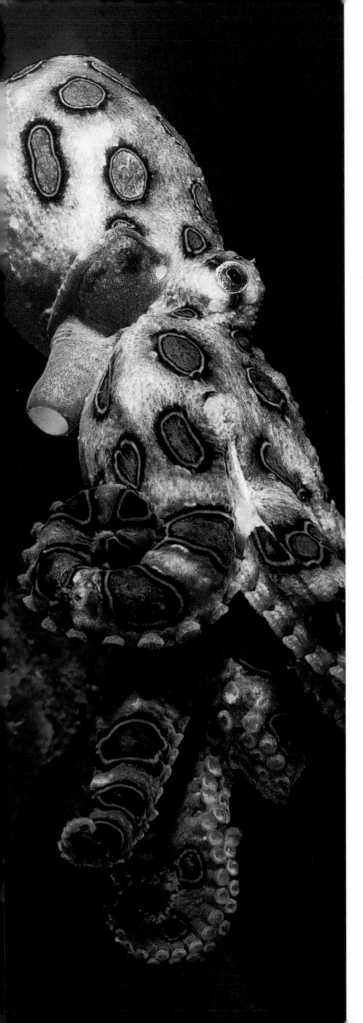

Thanks to the creative team:
Senior Editor: Alice Peebles
Designer: Lauren Woods and
collaborate agency
First published in Great Britain in 2015 by
Hungry Tomato Ltd
PO Box 181
Edenbridge
Kent, TN8 9DP

A CIP catalogue record for this book is available
from the British Library.
ISBN 978-1-910684-16-0

Printed and bound in China

Discover more at
www.hungrytomato.com

REAL-LIFE MONSTERS OF THE DEEP

By Matthew Rake

Illustrated by Simon Mendez

HUNGRY
TOMATO™

CONTENTS

MONSTERS OF THE DEEP

We live on a planet covered by 361 million sq km (139 million sq miles) of water. It makes up over 70% of the world's surface and, at its deepest, goes down a staggering 11km (6.8 miles). Have you ever thought what sort of monsters lurk in all that water? Well, you are about to find out. Most animals live at the top of the ocean where the sunlight can penetrate. However, in this book, we will go down to the cold, dark depths to find some of the most scary, sinister and downright ugly creatures on the planet.

No light can ever penetrate more than 1,000 m (3,280 ft) down, and below this lies the midnight zone. It's here, in mysterious darkness, that the goblin shark, many species of anglerfish and the blobfish all lurk. The goblin shark catches prey with its amazing jaws that catapult forward. The anglerfish goes for a more subtle approach: it lures prey towards it with what looks like a bait on the end of a fishing rod.

In the level above, about 200 to 1,000 m (650 ft to 3,280 ft) down, some sunlight penetrates the water, so this is known as the twilight zone. Here, the giant squid hangs out, ready to reach out its 10 m (33 ft) long tentacles to snatch any unsuspecting sea life passing by.

Great white sharks can also dive down into the twilight zone, although they generally live in the sunlight zone: the top 200 m (650 ft) of the water. Here, the great whites can find their favourite meal: juicy seals and sea lions. Killer whales also inhabit this zone, eating everything from other whales, dolphins and sharks to small fish, such as herring and salmon. Together the great whites and killer whales are the sea's top predators, like lions and tigers on the land.

In the sunlight zone, you will also find blue-ringed octopuses, cone snails, sarcastic fringeheads and moray eels, all living in reefs or close to the shore. The blue-ringed octopus, with its wonderful colour, and cone snails, with their pretty, patterned shells, might look harmless, but beware! They are two of the most poisonous creatures in the animal kingdom. And you don't want to go anywhere near a sarcastic fringehead or moray eel – they have razor sharp teeth and a powerful bite. Morays have even been known to bite off divers' fingers.

So if you're ready to plunge into the world of marine monsters, jump right in...

Length: up to 30 cm (12 in)
Weight: 9.5 kg (21 lb)
Location: off the shores of southeast Australia and New Zealand

Most fish have a swim bladder. This is simply a gas-filled organ inside the body that helps them stay buoyant. The blobfish, however, lives at depths of 600 to 1,200 m (2,000 to 3,900 ft) and the swim bladder doesn't work too well down there. The water pressure is over 100 times higher than at the surface, and the bladder, probably along with the fish, would simply explode. So instead of a swim bladder, the blobfish has goo-like flesh that is slightly less dense than water. It's a simple solution, allowing the fish to float above the bottom of the sea as if it were wearing a life-jacket.

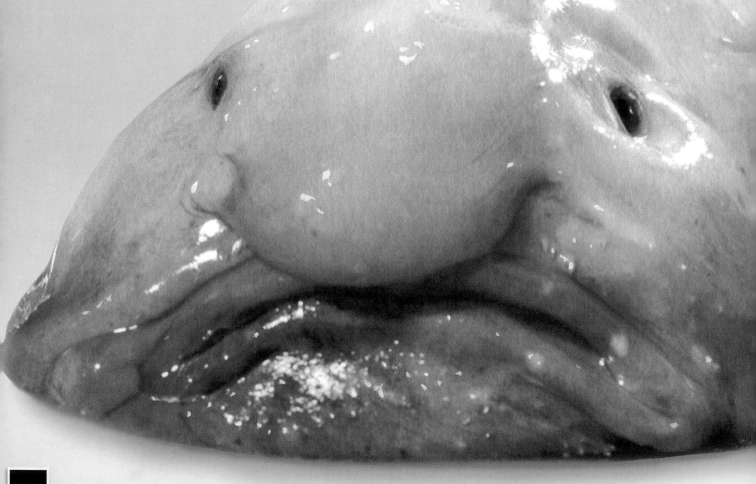

SINK OR SWIM – OR JUST FLOAT?

The blobfish's saggy, droopy flesh doesn't have much muscle, which, of course, means it can't swim fast to chase prey. So the blobfish simply floats above the sea floor and eats anything edible that appears in its way, such as crustaceans. There might not be huge amounts of food down in the depths, but there is enough for the blobfish, because it has no competition from fish with swim bladders.

UGLY CONTEST

In September 2013, the blobfish was voted the 'World's Ugliest Animal' at the British Science Festival. It was also adopted as the mascot of the Ugly Animal Preservation Society, whose motto is 'The panda gets too much attention.'

SIZE

2

POWER

1

STRENGTH

1

AGGRESSION

1

DEADLINESS

1

TOTAL

6

TOXIC TERROR

BLUE-RINGED OCTOPUS

Length: about 10 cm (4 in)
Weight: about 30–60 g (1–2 oz)
Location: around Australia, southeast Asia

With its beautiful colour and elegant curling arms, the blue-ringed octopus looks a pretty friendly creature. But, despite its small size, it carries enough venom to kill 26 adult humans within minutes. Its bite is often painless, with many human victims not even realizing they have been stung. In a matter of minutes, however, they can experience complete paralysis and death. Some who have survived say they were conscious, but unable to speak or move. So if you see a cute blue octopus on a beach, don't touch it!

LETHAL TOXIN

The blue-ringed octopus produces a poison called tetrodotoxin or TTX. Just one milligram of TTX can kill a person, so it is one of the most powerful natural toxins known. It is produced by bacteria in the octopus's salivary glands.

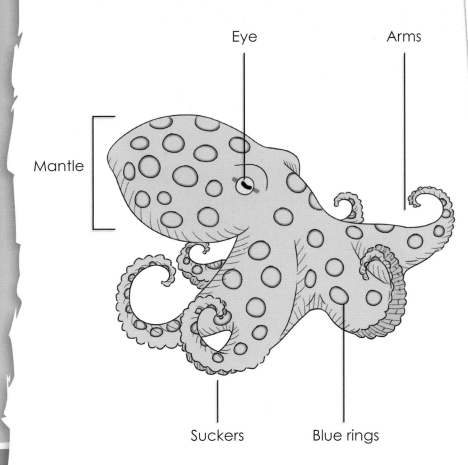

Mantle

Eye

Arms

Suckers

Blue rings

SHAPESHIFTING SKILLS

The blue-ringed octopus is so-named because its body darkens and the circles on its skin turn a brilliant blue to warn off predators, such as sharks and moray eels. The effect resembles a neon light. This octopus is not aggressive, though – it usually scuttles away into the reef if it senses danger. And it can get into virtually any crevice or hole. Like other octopuses, it has no skeleton, so it can squeeze into an opening no bigger than one of its eyeballs. It really is the ultimate shapeshifter.

SIZE

1

POWER

5

STRENGTH

3

AGGRESSION

8

DEADLINESS

7

TOTAL

24

8 SILENT ASSASSIN

CONE SNAIL

Weight: about 30 g (1 oz)
Length: 10 –15 cm (4 – 6 in)
Location: Indian and Pacific oceans,
the Caribbean and Red seas

Cone snails look quite harmless. They are small, live in pretty patterned shells and, like other snails, move very slowly so they can't chase anything. But appearances can be deceptive. Cone snails are, in fact, ruthless assassins. They can produce hundreds of toxins that they harpoon into their prey. It's instant paralysis and death for their victims.

TOXIN TREATMENTS

Today scientists are making pain-relief drugs from cone snail toxins. They estimat the toxins are 100 times more effective than the drugs currently used, such as morphine. Prialt is a drug made from the toxins of the species *Conus magus*, and this is given to treat the extreme pain suffered by cancer patients.

FISHING NET METHOD

1 The cone snail has two stalk eyes, a nose-like siphon and a mouth-like proboscis, all projecting from its shell. Its eyes aren't very effective, so the snail uses its siphon to smell prey. If it finds a fish, the snail extends its proboscis towards it – the proboscis can stretch to twice the length of its body if necessary.

2 Inside the proboscis is its secret weapon: a harpoon loaded with venom. When the cone snail fires this, the fish jerks rapidly for a second or two and then dies, turning as rigid as a board. As the harpoon is barbed, the snail reels the fish back into the proboscis to be eaten, like a fisherman reeling in his line!

3 The snail can take many hours or even days to digest the fish. Then it vomits out the bones, scales and harpoon, and reloads another harpoon. Luckily, it has around 20 harpoons growing inside so it always has another weapon to hand.

SIZE
2

POWER
2

STRENGTH
2

AGGRESSION
9

DEADLINESS
10

TOTAL
25

FISHING NET METHOD

Other cone snails use their proboscis like a fishing net. They open it wide so it looks like a tasty sea anemone or a hiding-place in the reef. Once a fish has comes to investigate, the cone snail closes the proboscis and harpoons the trapped prey inside the proboscis bubble.

SARCASTIC FRINGEHEAD

Length: up to 30 cm (12 in)
Weight: about 300g (10.5 oz)
Location: Pacific Ocean, from California to Mexico

What's this strangely named creature with the stretchy mouth? It's a fish – and it's called 'sarcastic' from the Greek word *sarkasmos* meaning 'to tear flesh'. And with that huge mouth full of needle-sharp teeth, it can really do some damage. But where does the fringehead part fit in? Well, check out those eyebrow-like tufts on its head.

GO IT ALONE

Sarcastic fringeheads are bitter old loners. Each one lives by itself in a discarded shell, a crevice in a rock, or even in an empty can or bottle – and it doesn't like intruders. It sticks its head out of its home to keep a watchful eye for anything or anyone venturing into its territory. At the first sign of a trespasser, it flexes and snaps its enormous jaws. If this doesn't work, it will attack. Sarcastic fringeheads go for almost anything that appears in their range of vision, including human divers! And their teeth can cut through wet suits. Fringeheads are particularly wary of other fringeheads as they will compete for the same food in their area. When two fringeheads have a territorial battle, they wrestle by pressing their huge mouths against each other, as if they were kissing. This allows them to determine which is the larger fish. The smaller fish will have to find another home well away from the larger one.

SIZE

3

POWER

4

STRENGTH

4

AGGRESSION

10

DEADLINESS

5

TOTAL

26

Length: 20 cm (8 in) up to 1 m (3 ft 3 in)
Weight: up to 50 kg (110 lb)
Location: Atlantic and Antarctic oceans

Ever heard of a fish that goes fishing? No? Well, meet the female anglerfish. She has her own personal fishing rod, which emerges straight out between her eyes. At the end is a fleshy growth that looks like a nice juicy animal swimming in the water, and glows in the darkness of the deep. When a passing fish or crustacean takes a bite at this growth, the anglerfish takes a bite at the fish. And what a bite! Her mouth matches the size of her head and is full of long, pointed teeth that are angled inwards, so there's no escape. The anglerfish can even extend her jaw and stomach to gobble up prey twice her size.

LIVING IN THE DARK

When living things create light, the process is known as bioluminescence. The anglerfish's bioluminescent growth is made by millions of bacteria. The bacteria get nutrients from the anglerfish, as well as a cool place to hang. And the anglerfish has a luminous bait at the end of her fishing rod – perfect for the dark depths of the ocean. When two organisms live closely together and depend on each other, like the anglerfish and the bacteria, it is known as a symbiotic relationship.

WHERE ARE THE MALES?

When scientists first discovered anglerfish, they wondered why all the specimens they captured were female. Then they noticed growths on many of them, and realized these were the male fish. A male anglerfish is tiny, with some only 6 mm (0.25 in) long. When he comes across a female, he bites into her skin so the two become fused together – for life! He loses all his internal organs, apart from the testes that hold the sperm. It's a perfect marriage: the male has no need to hunt for food, and the female has a partner to mate with when she is ready to reproduce.

SIZE

4

POWER

4

STRENGTH

4

AGGRESSION

8

DEADLINESS

7

TOTAL

27

Length: up to 4 m (13 ft – the slender giant moray)
Weight: up to 30 kg (66 lb – the giant moray)
Location: tropical and subtropical seas worldwide

The moray eel is no ordinary wriggler. It has two pairs of jaws, each with its own set of teeth. To grab its prey, it first bites normally with its mouth jaws, then the throat jaws come into play. They leap forward, bite down on the prey and pull it straight down the eel's gullet. Why does the moray have a second pair of jaws? They allow it to devour large animals within the narrow holes and crevices of the reef. Other predators don't even have room to open their mouths!

PREDATORY PARTNERS

The moray eel has a very special relationship with the grouper fish, the two species form a great hunting team. To get at fish hiding in reefs, the grouper visits the nearest moray, and performs a headshaking dance over its home. Usually the eel responds by following the grouper, which repeats the dance over the crevice where prey is hiding. The eel then moves in for the kill, while the grouper waits in the open water. Now there's no escape for the prey: if it hides in the reef, the eel eats it; if it bolts for open water, the grouper gets it.

SIZE

6

POWER

6

STRENGTH

6

AGGRESSION

5

DEADLINESS

5

TOTAL

28

ACTING ON IMPULSE

GOBLIN SHARK

Length: 3–4 m (10–13 ft)
Weight: up to 210 kg (460 lb)
Location: oceans worldwide

If you think this sinister-looking shark looks like a prehistoric monster, you wouldn't be far wrong. It's the last surviving member of the Mitsukurinidae family, which dates back to the days of the dinosaurs some 125 million years. Often called a 'living fossil', it's one of the world's most mysterious sharks. It lives deep in the ocean, as far down as 1,370 m (4,490 ft), so few have been caught and none have ever survived in public aquariums. However, the goblin shark may not be as rare as we think. In 2003, after an earthquake across the ocean floor near Taiwan, more than 100 goblin sharks were found by fishermen in just a few days.

A SIXTH SENSE

Appearances can be deceptive. The goblin shark's snout might look like a fearsome sword but it's actually soft and rubbery. It would be pretty useless in a fight, or even for rooting around in sand, but it's very good at detecting prey. It is packed with sensors (known as the ampullae of Lorenzini) that can detect the electrical fields that all animals give off. So, even though the goblin shark lives in the darkness of the deep ocean, it has no problem tracking down its next meal. It can even sense fish or crustaceans buried in the sand, or squid hidden in ink clouds.

HAMMERHEAD

Like the goblin shark, the hammerhead shark (right) also has a snout packed with special sensors that can detect the electrical fields of other animals. But the hammerhead's sensors are ranged across a wide, mallet-shaped snout, not a pointed one. This means it can scan large areas quickly, perfect for finding tasty stingrays hidden in the sand at the bottom of the sea.

SIZE	7
POWER	5
STRENGTH	5
AGGRESSION	8
DEADLINESS	7
TOTAL	32

The goblin shark has a unique way of catching its prey. Its jaws catapult forward suddenly, stretching almost to the end of its snout. And as the jaws open, the throat expands, too. This creates' a suction force that can hoover up all but the strongest-swimming prey.

TENTACLED TYRANT

GIANT SQUID

Length: 10 m (33 ft)
Weight: 200 kg (440 lb)
Location: oceans worldwide

No one has ever seen a fight between a sperm whale and a giant squid, but we know they happen because the beaks of giant squids have been found in the stomachs of dead sperm whales. And we know that the two animals must have massive fights because sperm whales are often covered with sucker marks and bite wounds from giant squids.

THIS IS REALLY SICK!

A sperm whale clearly enjoys eating all parts of a giant squid – except for the beak, which is too hard to digest. To get rid of the beak, the sperm whale produces ambergris. This is a slick, waxy substance that coats the beak and lets the whale safely vomit it up or poo it out. But it doesn't always work: 18,000 squid beaks were found in the stomach of one dead whale!

ATTACK AND DEVOUR

The giant squid eats fish and squid, including other giant squid. It spots prey with its huge eyes, which are the size of soccer balls. It then launches a surprise attack by shooting out its two 10-m (33-ft) feeding tentacles that are covered with hundreds of toothed suckers. The squid brings the prey up to its beak with the help of its eight arms. The razor-sharp beak breaks the food down into smaller pieces, and the radula, a tongue-like organ covered in teeth, grinds it down further. The food slides down its gullet, which – believe it or not – travels through the squid's doughnut-shaped brain to get to the stomach.

SIZE

7

POWER

7

STRENGTH

5

AGGRESSION

8

DEADLINESS

7

TOTAL

34

Length: up to 6 m (19 ft 8 in)
Weight: up to 3,000 kg (6,600 lb)
Location: temperate oceans worldwide

Torpedo-shaped and monster-sized, the great white shark rivals the killer whale as the most feared animal in the ocean. Its jaws are about 1 m (3ft 3in) wide and contain about 300 teeth. There are about 48 teeth in the front row, 24 at the bottom and 24 at the top. Behind, there are another five rows, each with about 48 teeth. This means that as soon as the shark loses any front teeth, they are replaced by ones from behind. In its 30-year lifetime, a shark can get through 30,000 to 50,000 teeth.

THE POLARIS

The great white relies on stealth and speed when hunting. One of its most spectacular hunting techniques is the vertical breach. The shark tracks the movement of its prey – usually a seal – by swimming close to the sea floor. While it follows the seal from below, the seal cannot pick out the shark's grey upper half against the sea floor. Once in position, the shark suddenly accelerates to the surface, moving at speeds of up to 56 km/h (35 mph). If all goes to plan, it will take the seal out before it propels itself out of the water. This move has been named 'the Polaris' after the submarine-launched missile.

SIZE

8

POWER

9

STRENGTH

9

AGGRESSION

10

DEADLINESS

9

TOTAL

45

1 LORD OF THE OCEAN

Length: up to 9.8 m (32 ft)
Weight: up to 10,000 kg (22,000 lb)
Location: oceans worldwide, from the Arctic to the Antarctic

KILLER WHALE

There is only one apex predator in the oceans and it isn't the great white shark. It's the killer whale, or orca. It will actually attack great whites, ramming them so they flip over and become unconscious and immobile. The killer whale's usual diet, however, is smaller sharks, penguins, sea turtles, squid and many fish, including rays, salmon and herring. For a decent-size meal, orcas will often attack sea mammals, such as seals, sea lions, walruses, dolphins and other whales. Working together in pods, orcas have been known to attack sperm whales, which are their fellow predators but about twice their weight, and even blue whales, which are 20 times heavier. Luckily, just about the only creatures they don't have a taste for are humans!

WAVE WASHING

1 You'd think a seal minding its own business on an ice floe would be pretty safe. It's well out of reach of any predators lurking in the water... or is it? This seal has not bargained for a pod of killer whales working as a team, using a fiendishly clever hunting strategy.

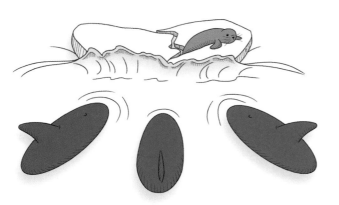

2 The killer whales swim side by side, rising and falling in unison, to create massive waves.

3 Eventually, they will create a wave big enough to topple the seal from its icy perch into the water. Then it's dinnertime.

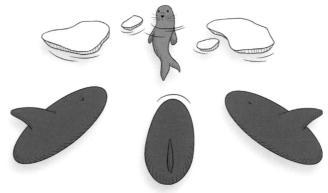

SIZE	9
POWER	9
STRENGTH	10
AGGRESSION	10
DEADLINESS	10
TOTAL	**48**

FAMILY AFFAIR

Orcas are not just ruthless killers. They have a friendly side, too. They live in pods or groups of 6 to 80 animals, and communicate with each other using echolocation: sending out click sounds. Each pod makes slightly different sounds, rather like humans who speak the same language but with different accents. Killer whales can recognize calls from members of their own pod from several kilometres away, so each one always knows where its companions are.

BLOBFISH

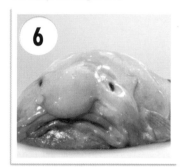

Down in the depths, the blobfish doesn't look quite as blobby as it does out of the water. Its jelly-like flesh is held together in a fish-like form by the pressure of water at the bottom of the ocean.

BLUE-RINGED OCTOPUS

The blue-ringed octopus litters the area in front of its nest with the shells and hollowed-out legs of the crustaceans it has eaten. It may put its rubbish out – but, unfortunately, in the sea there are no bin men to take it away!

ANGLERFISH

The anglerfish's fishing rod is known as the 'illicium' and the fleshy growth at the end is called the 'esca'. In some species, the illicium can be four or five times longer than the fish itself.

MORAY EEL

There are around 200 species of moray eel. The smallest moray is thought to be Snyder's moray, also known as the fine-spotted moray, which only grows up to 11.5 cm (4.5 in). It is found in the Pacific Ocean.

GREAT WHITE SHARK

A baby shark is called a pup. It grows from an egg that hatches in the mother's womb where it feeds on other unfertilized eggs. When the pup is born, it is about 1.5 m (5 ft) long and is immediately able to swim away from its mother and hunt for small marine animals on its own. Great whites don't reach maturity until 10-15 years old and can live up to 70 years.

CONE SNAIL

Some cone snails attack other molluscs rather than fish. Their venom causes the prey's muscles to go floppy, so it slips out of its shell and can be eaten easily. Other cone snails eat only worms. They are known as vermivores.

SARCASTIC FRINGEHEAD

Fringeheads are ambush predators, jumping out from their homes to surprise prey crawling or swimming by. Its huge mouth also allows it to eat animals nearly twice its own size, including octopuses.

GOBLIN SHARK

The goblin shark is not a fast swimmer, so scientists think it may be an ambush predator. Thanks to its low-density flesh and large oily liver, it can drift towards its prey without much movement and therefore avoids detection.

GIANT SQUID

Scientists first found colossal squids in the stomachs of dead sperm whales, deep in the ocean. A specimen caught off Antarctica in 2007 weighed 495 kg (1,091 lb), the heaviest squid ever found.

KILLER WHALE

In many countries, including the USA, Japan and Russia, orcas are kept in captivity. Many people say this is cruel because their tanks are small and nothing like their natural habitat. Orcas in captivity often act aggressively towards themselves, other orcas and humans. Critics point out that most don't live beyond 10 years, whereas in the wild, male orcas can live for 30 years and females for 50 years.

MORAY EEL

The moray eel is actually a shy, secretive creature. It makes its home in small crevices in reefs and only comes out at night. Most species do not have pectoral or pelvic fins on the sides of their bodies, so they are not good swimmers in open water and rarely venture away from the reef.

For this reason, diving companies have started hand-feeding morays so tourists can get a better look at them. Unfortunately, this also means divers occasionally lose fingers because morays have poor eyesight and find it hard to tell the difference between fingers and food!

CONE SNAIL

The geography cone, *conus geographus*, which lives off Australia, is the cone snail most lethal to humans and has caused several deaths. Its long, flexible proboscis can reach any part of its shell, which means it cannot be safely picked up by hand. The geography cone is nicknamed the 'cigarette snail', as any person it stings is believed to have time to smoke only one cigarette before dying. It's an exaggeration, but not a big one. One scientist has put the chances of surviving its venom at 30%. There is no cure; it's simply a question of trying to keep the victim alive until the toxins wear off.

GREAT WHITE SHARK

The great white shark has great eyesight for spotting prey. It is one of the few sharks to lift its head regularly above the water to look for prey. This is known as spy-hopping. It also has a strong sense of smell. Scientists think it can smell just one drop of blood floating in 10 billion drops of water! What's more, it can sense in what direction the drop of blood is located. Its two nostrils are widely spaced under the jaws. Smell coming from the left of the shark will arrive at the left nostril before the right one, so the shark will respond, by heading that way.

KILLER WHALE

Killer whales have various methods of catching their prey. In Argentina, they ride waves up to the shore to snatch sea lion pups off the beach, then roll back into the water on the next wave. Around New Zealand, they blow bubbles at eagle rays and stingrays to flush them out from the sediment on the sea floor.

Pods of orcas will also blow bubbles when they are herding schools of fish. And they dive under the school, flashing the white of their underbellies to stop the fish from escaping. Once they have fish in a tight bunch, some of the whales might swim through them, thrashing their tail flukes so the pod can feed off the stunned and injured fish. They might also force the fish on to a beach where they are easy to pick off.

INDEX

THE AUTHOR

Matthew Rake lives in London and has worked in publishing for more than twenty years. He has written on a wide variety of topics including science, sports, and the arts.

THE ARTIST

Award-winning illustrator Simon Mendez combines his love of nature and drawing by working as an illustrator with a focus on scientific and natural subjects. He paints on a wide variety of themes but mainly concentrates on portraits and animal subjects. He lives in the United Kingdom.

Picture Credits (abbreviations: t = top; b = bottom; c = centre; l = left; r = right)

© www.shutterstock.com: 2 l, 5 br, 7 br, 10 b, 12 b, 14 cl, 16 bl, 19 tr, 21 tr, 24 cl, 24 bl, 26 b, 28 tr, 28 cr, 28 bl, 29 tl, 29 tr, 29 bl, 30 tl, 30 b, 31 tr 31 bl.